PLACEHOLDER FOR OUTSIDE COVER PAGE

-DISCARD ONCE PRINTED-

Contact Us!

Dr. Nicki Newton

Email: gigglenook@gmail.com

Website: www.drnicki123.com

Blog: guidedmath.wordpress.com

Also by Dr. Nicki Newton

Guided Math in Action: Building Math Proficiency
Problem Solving With Math Models: Grade K
Problem Solving With Math Models: Grade 1
Problem Solving With Math Models: Grade 2
Problem Solving With Math Models: Grade 4
Problem Solving With Math Models: Grade 5

PROBLEM SOLVING™

WITH MATH MODELS

THIRD GRADE

DR. NICKI NEWTON

Giggle Nook Publications
Math with a Smile

Gigglenook Publication

P.O. Box 110134

Trumbull CT 06611

Email: gigglenook@gmail.com

Website: www.drnicki123.com

Produced by Gigglenook Publications

Thank you to the entire Production staff

Chief Operating Officer: Dr. Nicki Newton

Publisher: Gigglenook Publication

Cover Design: This Way Up Productions

Text Design and Composition: Bonnie Harrison-Jones

Printed in the United States of America

ISBN-13: 978-1493522255

ISBN-10: 1493522256

Volume 1: October, 2013

Dedicated to Mom and Pops, Always

TABLE OF CONTENTS

Foreword

Story problems can be great! Story problems are the stuff life is made of. If we can make connections for children between their daily lives and the problems we pose and solve in school, we will have much more success. We need to provide scaffolds into the process.

The New Math Common Core (CCSS ,2010) places a big emphasis on problem solving. The first mathematical practice mentioned states that students should "Make sense of problems and persevere in solving them." It goes on to describe this by stating that mathematically proficient students should be able to explain a problem and find ways to enter into it. According to the New Math Common Core students should be able to solve problems with objects, drawings and equations. In this book, students will practice word problems aligned to the standards by using the CCSS designated math models.

The Math Common Core, actually adopted the framework for story problems, created by Carpenter, Fennema, Franke, Levi & Empson, 1999; Peterson, Fennema & Carpenter (1989). The research says that the more teachers understand these types of problems and teach them to their students, the better students understand the problems and are able to solve them. Furthermore, the research makes the case that the KEY WORD METHOD should be avoided! Students should learn to understand the problem types and what they are actually discussing rather than "key word" tricks. The thing about key words is that they only work with really simplistic problems and so as students do more sophisticated work with word problems, the key words do not serve them well. They may actually lead them in the wrong direction, often encouraging the wrong operation. For example, given this problem: *John has 2 apples. Kate has 3 more than he does. How many do they have altogether?* Many students just add 2 and 3 instead of unpacking the problem. Another example, given this problem: *Sue has 10 marbles. She has 2 times as many marbles as Lucy. How many marbles does Lucy have?* Often times, students just multiply because they see the word times, instead of really reading and understanding the problem.

This book is about giving students a repertoire of tools, models and strategies to help them think about, understand and solve word problems. We want to scaffold reasoning opportunities from the concrete (using objects) to the pictorial (pictures and drawings) and, finally, to the abstract (writing equations).

DR. NICKI NEWTON

ACKNOWLEDGEMENTS

I would like to thank many people for their support, expertise, guidance, and encouragement during this project. First of all, I would like to thank God, without Him this would not be possible. Second, I would like to thank my mom, pa, big mom, and granddaddy. Third, I would like to thank my family for all their love and support, especially my Tia that calls me every day and asks, "What have you accomplished today?" And finally, I would like to thank all of my friends who support me all the time. This book series would not have been possible without the continual support of the Gigglenook Production Team. Thank you all!

Introduction to the Types of Problems

Grade Specific Problem Solving Expectations

The CCSS is very specific about what students should be able to do in terms of solving word problems by grade level. There are 4 general categories for addition and subtraction problems. In kindergarten students are exposed to 4 problem types - 1 addition, 1 subtraction, and 2 part/part whole problems. They are expected to work with these types of problems through 10. But, in first grade, there is a big leap. The standards say that the children will be able to work with the above-mentioned four problems, in addition to addition and subtraction change unknown problems, the other part/ part whole problem as well as comparison problems with unknowns in all positions and with a symbol for the unknown to represent the problem through 20. Students should also be able to solve word problems with three numbers adding up to 20. By second grade, they have to be able to solve all problem types, including the harder comparison problems through 100. In 3rd through 5th grade the students should be able to solve all of the problem types using larger whole numbers, fractions and decimals.

Adding to Problems

"Adding to" problems are all about adding. There are three types. The first type is *Adding to* problems where the result is unknown. For example, *Jenny had 5 marbles. John gave her 3 more. How many marbles does Jenny have now?* In this problem the result is unknown. Teachers tend to tell these types of problems. They are basic and straightforward. The teacher should start with concrete items, then proceed to drawing out the story, then to diagramming the story, and finally to using equations to represent the story. This is the easiest type of story problem to solve.

The second kind of *Adding to* problem is the "Change Unknown" problem. For example, *Jenny had 5 marbles. John gave her some more. Now she has 8 marbles. How many marbles did John give her?* In this type of problem, the students are looking for the change. They know the start and they know the end but they don't know the *change*. So, students have to put down the start and then count up to find how many. Students could also start with 8 marbles and take away the original 5 to see how many more were added to make 8.

The third type of *Adding to* Problem is a "Start Unknown" problem. For example, *Jenny had some marbles. John gave her 3 more. Now she has 8 marbles. How many marbles did Jenny have in the beginning?* In this type of problem, the students are looking for the start. This is the hardest type of *adding to* problem to solve. This takes a great deal of modeling.

Taking From Problems

Taking From problems are all about subtracting. There are three types. The first type is *taking from* problems where the result is unknown. For example, *Jenny had 5 marbles. She gave John 3. How many marbles does Jenny have left?* In this problem, the result is unknown. Teachers tend to tell these types of problems. They are basic and straightforward. The teacher should start with concrete items, then proceed to drawing out the story, then to diagramming the story, and finally to writing equations to represent the story.

The second kind of *Taking From* problem is the "Change Unknown" problem. For example, *Jenny had 10 marbles. She gave John some. Now she has 8 marbles left. How many marbles did she give to John?* In this type of problem, the students are looking for the change. They know the start and they know the end but they don't know the *change*. So, students have to put down the start and then count up to find how many. Students could also start with 10 marbles and take away some until they have 8 left. They would count to see how many they had to take away to remain with 8.

The third type of *Taking From* problem is a "Start Unknown" problem. For example, *Jenny had some marbles. She gave John 3. Now she has 7 marbles left. How many marbles did Jenny have to start with?* In this type of problem, the students are looking for the start. This is the hardest type of *taking from* problem to solve. This takes a great deal of modeling. You can use ten frames to show this. One strategy is to have the students put down the seven she has left and count up three to see how many that makes.

Part/Part Whole Problems

A *Part/Part Whole* problem is a problem that discusses the two parts and the whole. There are three types of *Part/Part Whole* Problems. The first is a problem where the *whole* is unknown. For example, *Susie has some marbles. Five are red and five are blue. How many marbles does she have altogether?* We know both parts and the task is to figure out the whole.

The second kind of problem is a problem where one of the *parts* is unknown. For example, *Susie has 10 marbles. Seven are red. The rest are blue. How many are blue?* In this type of problem, we are given the whole and one of the parts. The task is to figure out the other part.

The third type of problem is a *Both Addends Unknown* problem. In this type of problem both addends are not known, only the total is given. For example, *There are 4 frogs on the log. Some are blue and some are green. There are some of each color. How many of each color could there be?* The task is to figure out all the possible combinations.

Comparing Stories

Comparing Stories are the most difficult types of stories to tell. There are three types of comparison stories. The first type of comparison story is where two different things are being compared. For example, *Susie has ten lollipops and Kayla has eight. How many more lollipops does Susie have than Kayla?*

The second type of comparison story is where the bigger part is unknown. In this type of story, we are looking for the bigger amount. For example, *Susie had 4 candies. Maya had 3 more than her. How many candies did Maya have?* Here, we know what Susie had, and then in comparison, Maya had 3 more. The task is to find the bigger part.

The third type of comparison story is to find the smaller part. This is the hardest type of story to tell. For example, *Jaya has 7 candies. She has 3 more than Marcos. How many does Marcos have?* In this type of story we know what Jaya has and we know that she has 3 more than Marcos. We are looking for the smaller amount. We only know about what Marcos has in comparison to what Jaya has. The task is to use the information given to solve for the smaller part.

INTRODUCING THE MODELS FOR THINKING

◈ There are several great tools to use for solving number stories. In this book, students will use a few different tools to think about the word problems. The CCSSM Standards (2010) state that students should use "objects, drawings, diagrams and acting out" to solve problems. According to the CCSSM (2010)

3rd grade students should be able to:

USE EQUATIONS

◈ 3OA8: Solve two-step word problems **Represent these problems using equations with a letter standing for the unknown quantity**. Assess the reasonableness of answers using mental computation and estimation strategies including rounding.

USE INEQUALITIES

◈ 3NF3: Compare two fractions with the same numerator or the same denominator by reasoning about their size. Recognize that comparisons are valid only when the two fractions refer to the same whole. **Record the results of comparisons with the symbols >, =, or <, and justify the conclusions (e.g., by using a visual fraction model. ½ > ¼).**

USE OPEN NUMBERLINES

◈ 3MD1: Tell and write time to the nearest minute and measure time intervals in minutes. Solve word problems involving addition and subtraction of time intervals in minutes (**e.g., by representing the problem on a number line diagram**).

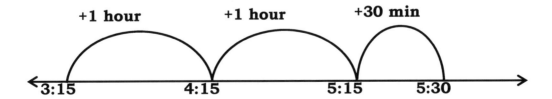

Students also use the open number line for other types of problems. They draw a line, plot numbers on it and count using a variety of strategies. For example, let's take the problem 45 plus 37.

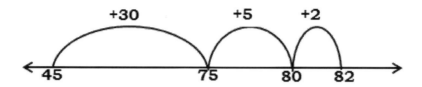

The student starts at 45 and jumps 30 because they broke apart the 37 into 30, plus 5, plus 2. From 75, they jump five more to 80 and then 2 more to 82. Number lines are a huge part of the new math CCSS and it is very important to make sure that students are very comfortable using them. Students will use number lines throughout the different grades.

DOUBLE OPEN NUMBER LINE

The double number line is a great model for comparing two different things. For example, *Sue had 15 apples and Josie had 4 more than she did. How many did Josie have?*

Students draw a line and then plot one part of the comparison on the top and the other part of the comparison on the bottom. (See below).

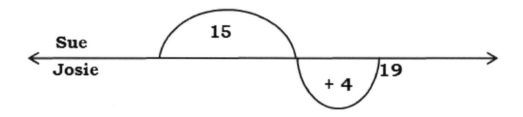

USE DRAWINGS

◈ 3MD2: Measure and estimate liquid volumes and masses of objects using standard units of grams (g), kilograms (kg), and liters (l). Add, subtract, multiply, or divide to solve one-step word problems involving masses or volumes that are given in the same units, (e.g., **by using drawings** such as a beaker with a measurement scale to represent the problem).

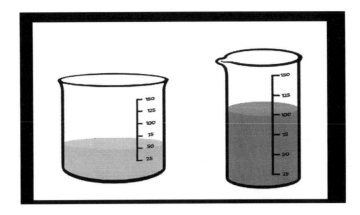

◈ **3MD3: Use data to draw a scaled picture graph and a scaled bar graph** to represent a data set with several categories. Solve one- and two-step "how many more" and "how many less" problems using information presented in scaled bar graphs.

The 3rd grade voted on their Favorite Animals. Use the data in the frequency table to make a bar graph.

Favorite Animals	
Birds	20
Cats	40
Dogs	50
Reptiles	30
Other	25

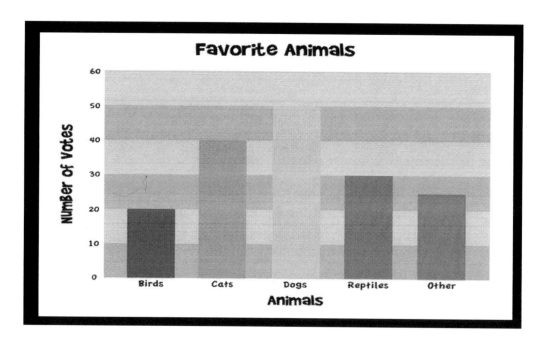

Questions:

1. How many people voted altogether?
2. How many more people liked cats than birds?
3. How many fewer people liked birds than dogs?

Problem Solving with Math Models© 2012

The 3rd grade voted on their favorite animals. Use the data in the frequency table to make a picture graph.

Favorite Animals	
Birds	20
Cats	40
Dogs	50
Reptiles	30
Other	25

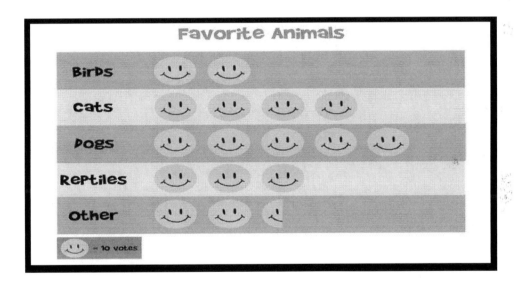

Questions:

1. How many people voted altogether?
2. How many more people liked cats than birds?
3. How many fewer people liked reptiles than liked dogs?

◆ 3MD4. Generate measurement data by measuring lengths using rulers marked with halves and fourths of an inch. Show the data by making a line plot, where the horizontal scale is marked off in appropriate units - whole numbers, halves, or quarters.

The 3rd grade made a frequency table of the length of their pet beetles. Use the data in the frequency table to make a line plot.

Length of baby beetles		
Type of Beetle	Number	Inches Long
Black Beetles	4	1
Orange Beetles	5	1 ½
Yellow Beetles	3	2

Line plot of pets per person in our classroom

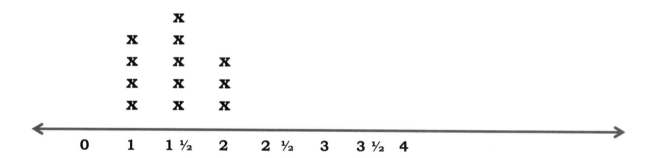

Line plot Questions:

1. How many pet beetles are there altogether?
2. What is the length of the longest beetle?
3. What is the length of the shortest beetle?

Problem Solving with Math Models© 2012

✤ **3MD8: Solve real world and mathematical problems involving perimeters of polygons**, including finding the perimeter given the side lengths, finding an unknown side length, and exhibiting rectangles with the same perimeter and different areas or with the same area and different perimeters.

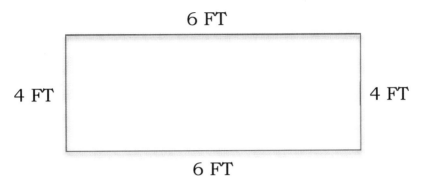

6 FT

4 FT   4 FT

6 FT

USE THE NUMBER GRID

The number grid is an excellent tool to help students develop efficient mental strategies. Students can initially use the number grid as a scaffold to break apart numbers, jump to friendly numbers and add or subtract quickly. For example, on the number grid to do *add to result unknown problems*, students choose a number to start with and then add. You want to teach them how to break apart numbers and use this method to add efficiently. For example, if the student has the numbers 45 plus 37 you want the student to know to count down 3 tens and then over 7.

1	2	3	4	5	6	7	8	9	10
11	12	13	14	15	16	17	18	19	20
21	22	23	24	25	26	27	28	29	30
31	32	33	34	35	36	37	38	39	40
41	42	43	44	45	46	47	48	49	50
51	52	53	54	55	56	57	58	59	60
61	62	63	64	65	66	67	68	69	70
71	72	73	74	75	76	77	78	79	80
81	82	83	84	85	86	87	88	89	90
91	92	93	94	95	96	97	98	99	100

USE BAR/TAPE DIAGRAM

In the CCSSM students are required to know how to use a tape diagram to model their thinking. *Bar diagrams help students to "unpack" the structure of a problem and lay the foundation for its solution"* (Diezmann *and English, 2001, p. 77 cited in Charles, Monograph 24324). Nickerson (1994) found that the ability to use diagrams is integral to mathematics thinking and learning (cited in Charles).*

In the charts below, I have provided a detailed explanation for each of the CCSS 1-step word problem types for addition and subtraction. The word problem type is designated with a sample problem. Then there is a bar diagram to show the relationships between the quantities. Then there is an explanation of the problem type and the various strategies that can be used to solve the problem. There is also the algebraic equation showing the different operations that can be used to solve the problem. As Charles (Monograph 24324) points out, *"It is important to recognize that a relationship in some word problems can be translated into more than one appropriate number sentence."*

Problem Solving with Math Models© 2012

Problem Types	Result Unknown	Change Unknown	Start Unknown
Join/Adding to	Marco had 5 marbles. His brother gave him 5 more. How many does he have now?	Marco had 5 marbles. His brother gave him some more. Now he has 10. How many did his brother give him?	Marco had some marbles. His brother gave him 5 more. Now he has 10. How many did he have in the beginning?
Bar Diagram Modeling Problem	? (5, 5)	10 (5, ?)	10 (?, 5)
What are we looking for? Where is X?	Both addends are known. We are looking for the total amount. The result is the unknown. In other words, we know what we started with and we know the change, we are looking for the end.	The first addend is known. The result is also known. We are looking for the change. The change is unknown. In other words, we know what happened at the start and we know what happened at the end. We are looking for the change. We need to find out what happened in the middle.	The second addend is known. The result is known. We are looking for the start. The start is unknown. In other words, we know the change and we know the end but we don't know what happened at the beginning.
Algebraic Sentence	$5 + 5 = ?$	$5 + ? = 10$ $10 - 5 = ?$	$x + 5 = 10$
Strategies to Solve	Add/ Know number Bonds/Know derived Facts/ Count Up	Count Up/Know Bonds/	Count up/Subtract
Answer	$5 + 5 = 10$ He had ten marbles.	$5 + 5 = 10$ $10 - 5 = 5$ He brother gave him five marbles.	$5 + 5 = 10$ $10 - 5 = 5$ He had five marbles.

Problem Types	Result Unknown	Change Unknown	Start Unknown
Separate/ Taking From	Marco had 10 marbles. He gave his brother 4. How many does he have left?	Marco had 10 marbles. He gave some away. Now he has 5 left. How many did he give away?	Marco had some marbles. He gave 2 away and now he has 5 left. How many did he have to start with?
Bar Diagram Modeling Problem	10 ←——————→ [4] [?]	10 ←——————→ [?] [5]	? ←——————→ [2] [5]
What are we looking for? Where is X?	In this story we know the beginning and what happened in the middle. The mystery is what happened at the end. The result is unknown.	In this story we know the beginning and the end. The mystery is what happened in the middle. The change is unknown.	In this story we know what happened in the middle and what happened at the end. The mystery is how did it start. start is unknown.
Algebraic Sentence	10 - 4 =?	10 – ? = 5 5 + x =10	? - 2 = 5 2 + 5 =?
Strategies to Solve	Subtract/ /Use number Bonds Facts/ Know derived Facts (Doubles -1, Doubles -2)	Subtract until you have the result left/ Count Up/Use number Bonds/Use derived facts	Count up/Subtract
Answer	10-4 = 6 He had 6 marbles left.	10-5=5 5 + 5 = 10 He gave away 5 marbles.	7-2=5 2+5=7 He had 7 marbles in the beginning.

Problem Solving with Math Models© 2012

Problem Types	Quantity Unknown	Part Unknown	Both Addends Unknown
Part/Part Whole/Putting together/Taking Apart	Marco has 5 red marbles and 5 blue ones. How many marbles does Marco have? $5 + 5 = x$	Marco has 10 marbles. Five are red and the rest are blue. How many are blue? $10 - 5 =$ or $5 + x = 10$	Marco has 10 marbles. Some are red and some are blue. How many could be red and how many could be blue?
Bar Diagram Modeling Problem	? ←————→ | 5 | 5 |	10 ←————→ | 5 | ? |	10 ←————→ | ? | ? |
What are we looking for? Where is X?	In this type of story we are talking about a group, set or collection of something. Here we know both parts and we are looking for the total.	In this type of story we are talking about a group, set or collection of something. Here we know the total and one of the parts. We are looking for the amount of the other part.	In this type of story we are talking about a group, set or collection of something. Here we know the total but we are to think about all the possible ways to make the group, set or collection.
Algebraic Sentence	$5 + 5 = ?$	$5 + ? = 10$ $10 - 5 = ?$	$x + y = 10$
Strategies to Solve	Add/ Know number Bonds/Know derived Facts/ Count Up	Count Up/Know Bonds/	Count up/Subtract
Answer	5+5=10 He had ten marbles.	5+5=10 10-5 =? Five were blue	1+9 4+6 9+1 6+4 2+8 5+5 8 + 2 3+7 10+0 0 +10 7+3 These are the possibilities

Problem Types	Difference Unknown	Bigger Part Unknown	Smaller Part Unknown
Compare	Marco has 5 marbles. His brother has 7. How many more marbles does his brother have than he does?	Marco has 5 marbles. His brother has 2 more than he does. How many marbles does his brother have?	Tom has 5 rocks. Marco has 2 less than Tom. How many rocks does Marco have?
Bar Diagram Modeling Problem			
What are we looking for? Where is X?	In this type of story we are comparing two amounts. We are looking for the difference between the two numbers.	In this type of story we are comparing two amounts. We are looking for the bigger part which is unknown.	In this type of story we are comparing two amounts. We are looking for the smaller part which is unknown.
Algebraic Sentence	$7-5=?$	$5+?=7$	$5-2=?$
Strategies to Solve	Count up/ Count back	Count up	Subtract
Answer	His brother had 2 more marbles than he did.	His brother had 7 marbles.	Marco had 3 marbles.

TEACHER TIPS :

- When you introduce the problem, be sure to tell the students what type of problem it is.

- Remember that you can take the same problem and rework it in different ways throughout the week.

- Work on a problem type until the students are proficient at recognizing and solving that problem type. Also, give them opportunities to write and tell what specific problem type it is.

- Be sure to contextualize the problems in the students' everyday lives. Using the problems in this book as models, substitute the students' names and everyday things.

- Be sure to provide tons of guided practice. Solve problems together as a class, with partners, and in groups. Individual practice should come after the students have had plenty of opportunities to work together and comprehend what they are doing.

- Emphasize that there is no one correct way to solve a problem, but that there is usually only one correct answer.

- Encourage students to always show their work

CHAPTER 1
ADD TO RESULT UNKNOWN PROBLEMS

These types of problems are the easiest types of addition problems. In these problems we know what happened in the beginning and we know what the change was but we do not know what happened in the end. We are trying to find out how many we have altogether.

PROBLEM	John had 10 marbles. Henry gave him 7 more. How many does he have now?
MODEL	
EQUATION	$10 + 7 = ?$ $\quad$ $10 + 7 = 17$

ADD TO RESULT UNKNOWN

1. Linda has 22 marbles. Dennis gave her 8 more, Maria gave her 9 more and Kate gave her 11 more. How many marbles does Linda have now?

Way#1: Solve with an open number line

Way#2: Represent the problem using letters for the unknown quantity. Solve with numbers.

Explain your thinking:

ADD TO RESULT UNKNOWN

2. Brian left his house at 2:15 p.m. He spent an hour at Ted's house and an hour at the basketball court and then he went home. What time did Brian go home?

Way#1: Represent the problem on a number line diagram.

Way#2: Write the answer

Explain your thinking:

ADD TO RESULT UNKNOWN

3. Lauren the baker used 57 grams of sugar in the cake mixture. Then she added 28 more grams of sugar. How many grams of sugar did she use altogether?

Way#1: Solve with a number grid

1	2	3	4	5	6	7	8	9	10
11	12	13	14	15	16	17	18	19	20
21	22	23	24	25	26	27	28	29	30
31	32	33	34	35	36	37	38	39	40
41	42	43	44	45	46	47	48	49	50
51	52	53	54	55	56	57	58	59	60
61	62	63	64	65	66	67	68	69	70
71	72	73	74	75	76	77	78	79	80
81	82	83	84	85	86	87	88	89	90
91	92	93	94	95	96	97	98	99	100

Way#2: Represent the problem using letters for the unknown quantity. Solve with numbers.

Explain your thinking:

ADD TO RESULT UNKNOWN

4. Andres made fruit punch. First, he put in 29 ml of cranberry juice, then he added 58 ml of pineapple juice, then he added 12 ml of banana juice. How many ml of juice did Andres put in the fruit punch altogether?

Way#1: Solve with a number grid

1	2	3	4	5	6	7	8	9	10
11	12	13	14	15	16	17	18	19	20
21	22	23	24	25	26	27	28	29	30
31	32	33	34	35	36	37	38	39	40
41	42	43	44	45	46	47	48	49	50
51	52	53	54	55	56	57	58	59	60
61	62	63	64	65	66	67	68	69	70
71	72	73	74	75	76	77	78	79	80
81	82	83	84	85	86	87	88	89	90
91	92	93	94	95	96	97	98	99	100

Way#2: Represent the problem using letters for the unknown quantity. Solve with numbers.

Explain your thinking:

Problem Solving with Math Models© 2012

ADD TO RESULT UNKNOWN

5. Jason made a small fruit juice drink for breakfast. First, he added 50 ml of apple juice and then he added 25 ml of pineapple juice. How many ml of juice did Jason make?

Way#1: Solve with a drawing

Way#2: Represent the problem using letters for the unknown quantity. Solve with numbers.

Explain your thinking:

ADD TO RESULT UNKNOWN

6. The candy store made 459 grams of chocolate fudge in the morning. In the afternoon, they made 378 more grams. How many grams did they make altogether?

Way#1: Model with a tape diagram

Way#2: Represent the problem using letters for the unknown quantity. Solve with numbers.

Explain your thinking:

ADD TO RESULT UNKNOWN

7.   Farmer John built a yard for his chickens to run around in. It was 5 ft. long and 5 ft. wide. He found it to be too short. So he added 8 more feet to the length.   What was the length of the fence with the addition?   What was the perimeter of the fence with the addition?

Way#1: Draw an illustration to solve

Way#2: Show all your mathematical thinking

Explain your thinking:

ADD TO RESULT UNKNOWN

8. Shakhira made necklaces. She used 67 inches of string and then bought 89 more inches Monday night. Tuesday morning, she bought 55 more inches and on Wednesday morning she bought 108 more inches. How much string did Shakhira buy altogether?

Way#1: Model with a tape diagram

Way#2: Represent the problem using letters for the unknown quantity. Solve with numbers.

Explain your thinking:

CHAPTER 1 QUIZ:
ADD TO RESULT UNKNOWN

Solve with a model:

1. Grandma Nola is baking pies. They need to bake for 1 and a half hours. She put them in the oven at 12:15. What time should she take them out of the oven?

2. Farmer Jenny built a rabbit cage. She made the length 5ft. and the width 5ft. Then she decided to add 4 more feet to each side. What is the new perimeter of the cage?

3. The candy store had 399 gumballs. On Monday, they got 234 more gumballs and on Tuesday they got 288 more. How many gumballs do they have now?

4. The bakery had 15 kilograms of chocolate. They bought 19 more kilograms. How much chocolate do they have now?

CHAPTER 2
ADD TO CHANGE UNKNOWN PROBLEMS

In these problems, students are looking for what happened in the middle of the story. In this type of story, we know what happened at the beginning but then some change happened and now we have more than we started with. We are trying to find out how many things were added in the middle of the story.

PROBLEM	John had 5 marbles. His mother gave him some more. Now he has 12. How many did his mother give him?
MODEL	
EQUATION	$5 + ? = 12$ $\qquad$ $5 + 7 = 12$

ADD TO CHANGE UNKNOWN

1. Adrian had 55 marbles. His brother gave him ten more. Then, his sister gave him some too. Now he has 80 marbles. How many did his sister give him?

Way#1: Solve with an open number line

Way#2: Represent the problem using letters for the unknown quantity. Solve with numbers.

Explain your thinking:

ADD TO CHANGE UNKNOWN

2. Jose went to the basketball court at 2:15 p.m. He was there for a while and then he went home. He went home at 3:15 p.m. How long was he at the basketball court?

Solve with a number line diagram.

Explain your thinking:

ADD TO CHANGE UNKNOWN

3. Mr. Kaku used 250 grams of powdered chocolate to make some cookies. Then he added some more to the mix. Altogether he used 500 grams of powdered chocolate. How much did he add to the mix?

Way#1: Model with a tape diagram

Way#2: Represent the problem using letters for the unknown quantity. Solve with numbers.

Explain your thinking:

Problem Solving with Math Models© 2012

ADD TO CHANGE UNKNOWN

4. Deon made fruit punch for a party. He used 200 ml of cherry juice and then he added some apple juice. Altogether he used 700 ml of juice. How much apple juice did he add?

Way#1: Draw a picture of a beaker to solve

Way#2: Represent the problem using letters for the unknown quantity. Solve with numbers.

Explain your thinking:

ADD TO CHANGE UNKNOWN

5.   Clare had 56 stickers. Her mom gave her 14 more, her dad gave her 12 more, and her brother gave her some. Now she has 100. How many did her brother give her?

Way#1: Solve with a number grid

1	2	3	4	5	6	7	8	9	10
11	12	13	14	15	16	17	18	19	20
21	22	23	24	25	26	27	28	29	30
31	32	33	34	35	36	37	38	39	40
41	42	43	44	45	46	47	48	49	50
51	52	53	54	55	56	57	58	59	60
61	62	63	64	65	66	67	68	69	70
71	72	73	74	75	76	77	78	79	80
81	82	83	84	85	86	87	88	89	90
91	92	93	94	95	96	97	98	99	100

Way#2: Represent the problem using letters for the unknown quantity. Solve with numbers.

Explain your thinking:

ADD TO CHANGE UNKNOWN

6. In the jumping competition, Kara jumped 48 centimeters for her first jump and then some more centimeters for her second jump. Altogether she jumped 100 centimeters. How many centimeters did she jump for her second jump?

Way#1: Solve with an open number line

Way#2: Represent the problem using letters for the unknown quantity. Solve with numbers.

Explain your thinking:

ADD TO CHANGE UNKNOWN

7. Farmer Jane built a yard for her rabbits. First, she made a yard that was 5 ft. long and 7 ft. wide. Then she added some fence to the length. Now the length of the fence is 9 ft. How much fence did she add to the length? What is the new perimeter of the yard?

Way#1: Solve with drawing

Way#2: Show all your mathematical thinking

Explain your thinking:

ADD TO CHANGE UNKNOWN

8. A toy store had 18 action figures. They got 34 more on Tuesday. On Wednesday, they got another shipment and now they have 105. How many did they get on Wednesday?

Way#1: Solve with an open number line

Way#2: Represent the problem using letters for the unknown quantity. Solve with numbers.

Explain your thinking:

CHAPTER 2 QUIZ: ADD TO CHANGE UNKNOWN PROBLEMS

Solve with a model:

1. Mary put 250 ml of milk in the cake recipe and then she added some more. Altogether she added a total 307 ml of milk to the recipe. How much more milk did she add to the original amount?

2. The pizza shack had 28 kilograms of shredded cheese. They got some more and now they have 52 kilograms. How much shredded cheese did they get?

3. The bakery baked 27 cupcakes in the morning. In the afternoon they baked 39 more. In the evening, they baked some more. In total, they baked 81 cupcakes. How many more did they bake in the evening?

4. Kelly left her house at 2:25 p.m. She went to the mall for an hour. Then she went to her friend's house. She came home at 4:25 p.m. How long was she at her friend's house?

CHAPTER 3
ADD TO START UNKNOWN PROBLEMS

In these problems, students are looking for what happened in the beginning of the story. In this type of story, we know what happened in the middle and we know how many we ended up with, but we are looking for how the story started.

PROBLEM	John had some marbles. Henry gave him 7 more. Now he has 14. How many did he have in the beginning?
MODEL	
EQUATION	? + 7 = 14 7 + 7 = 14

ADD TO START UNKNOWN

1.   Danielle had some gummy bears. Samantha gave her 15 more. Now she has 30 gummy bears. How many gummy bears did she have to start with?

Way#1: Model with a tape diagram

Way#2: Represent the problem using letters for the unknown quantity. Solve with numbers.

Explain your thinking:

ADD TO START UNKNOWN

2.   Ethan went to the mall for 2 hours. He then went to his friend's house for 1 hour. He came back to his house at 3:15 p.m. What time did he leave his house originally?

Solve with a number line diagram

Explain your thinking:

ADD TO START UNKNOWN

3. Farmer Dawn built a fence around her farm. She added 30 more feet to the length of the original fence and now it is 45 feet long. How long was the original fence?

Way#1: Model with a tape diagram

Way#2: Show your calculations

Explain your thinking:

ADD TO START UNKNOWN

4. The candy store had some fudge. They got a shipment of 25 more kilograms and now they have 50 kilograms. How much fudge did they have in the beginning?

Way#1: Solve with a number grid

1	2	3	4	5	6	7	8	9	10
11	12	13	14	15	16	17	18	19	20
21	22	23	24	25	26	27	28	29	30
31	32	33	34	35	36	37	38	39	40
41	42	43	44	45	46	47	48	49	50
51	52	53	54	55	56	57	58	59	60
61	62	63	64	65	66	67	68	69	70
71	72	73	74	75	76	77	78	79	80
81	82	83	84	85	86	87	88	89	90
91	92	93	94	95	96	97	98	99	100

Way#2: Represent the problem using letters for the unknown quantity. Solve with numbers.

Explain your thinking:

ADD TO START UNKNOWN

5. The school cook made some liters of fruit punch. He then made 12 more liters. Altogether he made 50 liters of fruit punch. How much fruit punch did he make in the beginning?

Way#1: Model with a tape diagram

Way#2: Represent the problem using letters for the unknown quantity. Solve with numbers.

Explain your thinking:

ADD TO START UNKNOWN

6. Jason had some marbles. Walter gave him 19 more. His sister gave him 22 more. Now he has 74 marbles. How many marbles did he have to start?

Way#1: Solve with a number line

Way#2: Represent the problem using letters for the unknown quantity. Solve with numbers.

Explain your thinking:

ADD TO START UNKNOWN

7. The fruit stand sold some kilograms of apples in the morning, 35 kilograms of apples in the afternoon and 38 more in the evening. Altogether they sold 81 kilos of apples. How many did they sell in the morning?

Way#1: Solve with an open number line

Way#2: Represent the problem using letters for the unknown quantity. Solve with numbers.

Explain your thinking:

ADD TO START UNKNOWN

8. The circus had some stuffed animals. They got a shipment of 39 more and now they have 84. How many did they have in the beginning?

Way#1: Solve with an open number line

Way#2: Represent the problem using letters for the unknown quantity. Solve with numbers.

Explain your thinking:

Problem Solving with Math Models© 2012

CHAPTER 3 QUIZ:
ADD TO START UNKNOWN PROBLEMS

Show your mathematical thinking:

1. Kelly had some string to make bracelets. She bought 99 more centimeters of string. Now she has 205 centimeters of string. How much string did she have in the beginning?

2. Jamal left his house early in the morning. He went to his grandmother's for 3 hours. Then he went to his cousin's house for another hour. He came home at 11:25 a.m. What time did he leave his house in the morning?

3. Chef Marcus made a fancy soup. He put in some coconut juice and then he added another 256 ml of coconut juice. Altogether he used 407 ml of coconut juice. How much coconut juice did he put in the fancy soup in the beginning?

4. Cleo ran on Monday morning. On Tuesday, she ran 3 more kilometers. On Wednesday, she ran another 2 kilometers. Altogether she ran 7 kilometers. How many kilometers did she run on Monday morning?

Unit 1 Test:
Addition Problems

Solve with a model:

1. The jewelry store had 87 rings. They got a shipment of 35 more on Monday, 54 more on Tuesday, and 56 more on Wednesday. How many rings do they have now?

2. Raul had 25 marbles. He bought 17 more. His sister then gave him some more. Now he has 55 marbles. How many did his sister give him?

3. The bakery made 48 cookies in the morning and 34 more cookies in the afternoon. They also made some in the evening. Now they have 100 cookies. How many did they make in the evening?

4. Marvin, the baker, made some fudge. He used some sugar to start with and then he added 345 more grams of sugar. He used 500 grams of sugar altogether. How much did he use in the beginning?

CHAPTER 1
TAKE FROM RESULT UNKNOWN PROBLEMS

In these problems, students are looking for what happened in the end of the story. In this type of story, we know what happened at the beginning and also what change occurred. We are trying to find out how many things remained after some things were taken away.

PROBLEM	John had 10 apples. He gave 5 away. How many does he have left?
MODEL	
EQUATION	$10 - ? = 5$

TAKE FROM RESULT UNKNOWN

1. Daniel had $352. He paid $55 for some shoes. He paid $38 for some videos and he paid $209 for some clothes. How much did he have left?

Way#1: Solve with an open number line

Way#2: Show all your mathematical thinking

Explain your thinking:

TAKE FROM RESULT UNKNOWN

2. Baker Maria had 25 kilograms of fudge. She sold 8 kilograms in the morning, 12 kilograms in the afternoon, and 2 more kilograms in the evening. How many kilograms does she have left?

Way#1: Solve with a number line

Way#2: Show all your mathematical thinking

Explain your thinking:

TAKE FROM RESULT UNKNOWN

3.   Sara had 305 cm of string to make bracelets. She used 98 cm on Monday, 36 cm on Tuesday, 48 cm on Wednesday, and 104 cm on Thursday. How much string did she have left on Friday?

Way#1: Model with a tape diagram

Way#2: Show your calculations

Explain your thinking:

TAKE FROM RESULT UNKNOWN

4. Tamera had 100 butterfly stamps. She gave 8 to her cousin, 9 to her sister and 7 to her friend. She also used 28 stamps. How many stamps does she have left?

Way#1: Solve with a number grid

1	2	3	4	5	6	7	8	9	10
11	12	13	14	15	16	17	18	19	20
21	22	23	24	25	26	27	28	29	30
31	32	33	34	35	36	37	38	39	40
41	42	43	44	45	46	47	48	49	50
51	52	53	54	55	56	57	58	59	60
61	62	63	64	65	66	67	68	69	70
71	72	73	74	75	76	77	78	79	80
81	82	83	84	85	86	87	88	89	90
91	92	93	94	95	96	97	98	99	100

Way#2: Show all your mathematical thinking

Explain your thinking:

TAKE FROM RESULT UNKNOWN

5. Benjamin had 450 pages to read. He read 100 on Monday, 55 on Tuesday, 38 on Wednesday, and 89 on Thursday. How many more pages does he have to read to finish the book?

Way#1: Solve with an open number line

Way#2: Show your calculations

Explain your thinking:

Problem Solving with Math Models© 2012

TAKE FROM RESULT UNKNOWN

6. Claire wanted to exercise for 1 hour. She ran for 15 minutes. She biked for a half of an hour. How much longer does she have to exercise?

Solve with a number line diagram

Explain your thinking:

TAKE FROM RESULT UNKNOWN

7. There were 1000 ml of milk in the refrigerator. Jose drank 487 ml in the morning and then 438 ml in the afternoon. How many ml were left?

Solve with a number line diagram

Explain your thinking:

TAKE FROM RESULT UNKNOWN

8.   Grace had a square fence with a perimeter of 20 feet. She had to shorten the yard so she took away 2 feet from each side. What is the perimeter of the fence now?

Draw a picture to solve

Explain your thinking:

CHAPTER 1 QUIZ:
TAKE FROM RESULT UNKNOWN PROBLEMS

Solve with a model:

1. The bakery had 200 cookies. They sold 44 in the morning, 55 in the afternoon, and 46 in the evening. How many cookies do they have left?

2. The fruit stand had 20 kilograms of apples. They sold half in the morning and 3 more kilograms in the afternoon. How many kilograms of apples did they have left?

3. Lucinda had 100 centimeters of string. She used 43 centimeters to make a necklace and 15 centimeters to make a bracelet. How much string did she have left?

4. Kelly had $500. She spent $199 on shoes, $44 on jewelry, and $249 on clothes. How much does she have left?

CHAPTER 2
TAKE FROM CHANGE UNKNOWN PROBLEMS

In these problems, students are looking for what happened in the middle of the story. In this type of story, we know what happened at the beginning but then some change happened and, by the end of the story, we have less than what we started with. We are trying to find out how many things were taken away in the middle of the story.

PROBLEM	John had 15 marbles. He gave some to his cousin. Now he has 12 left. How many did he give to his cousin?
MODEL	
EQUATION	15 – ? = 12 15 - 3 =12

TAKE FROM CHANGE UNKNOWN

1. The fruit stand sold 25 kilos of apples. They sold 9 in the morning, 12 in the afternoon and some more in the evening. How many did they sell in the evening?

Way#1: Solve with a number line

Way#2: Represent the problem using letters for the unknown quantity. Solve with numbers.

Explain your thinking:

TAKE FROM CHANGE UNKNOWN

2. Claire left her house at 8:15 a.m. She came back at 9:30 a.m. How long was she gone?

Solve with a number line diagram

Explain your thinking:

Problem Solving with Math Models© 2012

TAKE FROM CHANGE UNKNOWN

3. Tom left his house at 4:25 p.m. He came back at 7:05 p.m. How long was he gone?

Solve with an number line diagram

Explain your thinking:

TAKE FROM CHANGE UNKNOWN

4.   The candy store sold 40 kilos of chocolate candy. They sold 19 kilos in the morning, some in the afternoon and 10 in the evening. How much did they sell in the afternoon?

Way#1: Solve with a number grid

1	2	3	4	5	6	7	8	9	10
11	12	13	14	15	16	17	18	19	20
21	22	23	24	25	26	27	28	29	30
31	32	33	34	35	36	37	38	39	40
41	42	43	44	45	46	47	48	49	50
51	52	53	54	55	56	57	58	59	60
61	62	63	64	65	66	67	68	69	70
71	72	73	74	75	76	77	78	79	80
81	82	83	84	85	86	87	88	89	90
91	92	93	94	95	96	97	98	99	100

Way#2: Represent the problem using letters for the unknown quantity. Solve with numbers.

Explain your thinking:

TAKE FROM CHANGE UNKNOWN

5. The store had 542 cm of string for sale. One customer bought 225 cm, another customer bought 37 cm, and a third customer bought some as well. Altogether the store sold 300 cm of string. How much did customer 3 buy? How much does the store have left?

Way#1: Model with a tape diagram

Way#2: Show all your mathematical thinking

Explain Your Thinking:

TAKE FROM CHANGE UNKNOWN

6. The length of a fence was originally 15 ft. long. The width was 10 feet long. Dan shortened the fence. Now it is only 7 ft. long. By how much did Dan shorten the fence? What is the new perimeter?

Way#1: Solve with a drawing

Way#2: Show all your mathematical thinking

Explain your thinking:

TAKE FROM CHANGE UNKNOWN

7. The perimeter of the rabbit yard was 5 ft. long and 8 ft. wide. Carla shortened the width to be 5 ft. wide. By how much did Carla shorten the width? What is the new perimeter of the fence?

Way#1: Solve with a drawing

Way#2: Show all your mathematical thinking

Explain your thinking:

TAKE FROM CHANGE UNKNOWN

8. Lucy had $208. She spent $55 on shoes, $87 on clothes and some on jewelry. She spent $189 total. How much did she spend on jewelry? How much does she have left?

Way#1: Solve with an open number line

Way#2: Represent the problem using letters for the unknown quantity. Solve with numbers.

Explain your thinking:

CHAPTER 2 QUIZ:
TAKE FROM CHANGE UNKNOWN PROBLEMS

Solve with a model:

1. Mark had 107 marbles. He gave 17 to his brother, 15 to his cousin, and some to his friend. He gave a total of 40 marbles away. How many did he give to his friend? How many does he have left?

2. Baker Francisco had 40 kilos of sugar. During the week, he used 12 kilos in some cakes, 15 kilos in some cookies and some sugar in the brownies. He used 35 kilos total. How much did he use in the brownies?

3. Mr. Lee left his house at 3:07 p.m. He came back at 5:12 p.m. How long was he gone?

4. Tamara had $91. She spent $27 on jewelry, $28 on clothes, and some money on shoes. She spent $82 total. How much did she spend on shoes? How much did she have left?

CHAPTER 3
TAKE FROM START UNKNOWN PROBLEMS

In these problems, students are looking for how many things there were at the beginning of the story. In this type of story, we only know that there was some amount and that there was a change (some things were taken away). We know what was taken away and how much was left. We are trying to find out how much we had in the beginning of the story.

PROBLEM	John had some marbles. He gave his brother 5. Now he has 10 left. How many did he have in the beginning?
MODEL	
EQUATION	? - 5 = 10 15 – 5 = 10

TAKE FROM START UNKNOWN

1. Claire spent $34 on shoes, $56 on clothes, and $28 on jewelry. She had $15 left. How much did she have in the beginning?

Way#1: Model with a tape diagram

Way#2: Represent the problem using letters for the unknown quantity. Solve with numbers.

Explain your thinking:

TAKE FROM START UNKNOWN

2. Sean drank some milk in the morning. He drank 500 ml of milk in the afternoon and 250 ml of milk in the evening. Altogether, he drank 900 ml of milk. How much did he drink in the morning?

Way#1: Solve with a drawing

Way#2: Represent the problem using letters for the unknown quantity. Solve with numbers.

Explain your thinking:

TAKE FROM START UNKNOWN

3.   The bakery had some cookies. They sold 74 and now they have 22 left. How many did they have to start?

Way#1: Solve with a number grid

1	2	3	4	5	6	7	8	9	10
11	12	13	14	15	16	17	18	19	20
21	22	23	24	25	26	27	28	29	30
31	32	33	34	35	36	37	38	39	40
41	42	43	44	45	46	47	48	49	50
51	52	53	54	55	56	57	58	59	60
61	62	63	64	65	66	67	68	69	70
71	72	73	74	75	76	77	78	79	80
81	82	83	84	85	86	87	88	89	90
91	92	93	94	95	96	97	98	99	100

Way#2: Represent the problem using letters for the unknown quantity. Solve with numbers.

Explain your thinking:

Problem Solving with Math Models© 2012

TAKE FROM START UNKNOWN

4.   The clothing store had some sweaters. They sold 19 on Monday, 28 on Tuesday, and 46 on Wednesday. Now they have 23 left. How many did they have to start?

Way#1: Solve with a number line

Way#2: Represent the problem using letters for the unknown quantity. Solve with numbers.

Explain your thinking:

TAKE FROM START UNKNOWN

5. Quincy had some marbles. He gave Hong 19 marbles. He gave his brother 19 as well. Now he has 46 marbles. How many marbles did he have to start?

Way#1: Model with a tape diagram

Way#2: Represent the problem using letters for the unknown quantity. Solve with numbers.

Explain your thinking:

Problem Solving with Math Models© 2012

TAKE FROM START UNKNOWN

6. Jessica had some string. She used 25 cm to make a bracelet and 50 cm to make a necklace. She has 25 cm left. How much did she have in the beginning?

Way#1: Solve with an open number line

Way#2: Represent the problem using letters for the unknown quantity. Solve with numbers.

Explain your thinking:

TAKE FROM START UNKNOWN

7. The candy store sold 5 kilos of candy on Monday, 10 kilos of candy on Tuesday, and 12 kilos of candy on Wednesday. They have 15 kilos of candy left. How many kilos did they have in the beginning?

Way#1: Solve with an open number line

Way#2: Represent the problem using letters for the unknown quantity. Solve with numbers.

Explain your thinking:

3. The jewelry store had 102 rings. They sold 55 on Monday, 16 on Tuesday, and some on Wednesday. They sold a total of 90 rings. How many did they sell on Wednesday? How many did the jewelry store have left?

4. Kelly arrived at the mall at 3:10 p.m. She left her house 25 minutes earlier. What time did she leave her house?

CHAPTER 1
PUT TOGETHER/TAKE APART PROBLEMS

These types of problems are about sets of things. In them, we know both parts and we are looking for the whole. What distinguishes a Put Together/Take Apart Problem from an Add to Result Unknown problem is *action*. In a Put together/Take Apart Problem, there is no action; there is only a set of something.

PROBLEM	John had five red apples and five green ones. How many apples did he have altogether?
MODEL	
EQUATION	5 + 5 = ? 5 + 5 = 10

PUT TOGETHER/TAKE APART—WHOLE UNKNOWN

1. The toy store had 129 toy cars and 157 toy trucks. How many vehicles did they have altogether?

Way#1: Solve with an open number line

Way#2: Represent the problem using letters for the unknown quantity. Solve with numbers.

Explain your thinking:

PUT TOGETHER/TAKE APART—WHOLE UNKNOWN

2. Sue built a fence. The length was 8 ft. The width was 5 ft. What was the perimeter?

Way#1: Solve with a drawing

Way#2: Show all your mathematical thinking

Explain your thinking:

PUT TOGETHER/TAKE APART—WHOLE UNKNOWN

3. Tom left his house at 3:30 p.m. He played soccer for 1 hour and 45 minutes and then he played basketball for 2 hours and 30 minutes. How long did he play sports? What time did he stop playing?

Solve with a number line diagram

Explain your thinking:

PUT TOGETHER/TAKE APART—WHOLE UNKNOWN

4. Sue biked 5 miles on Monday, 7 miles on Tuesday, 4 miles on Wednesday, and 7 miles on Thursday. How many miles did she ride altogether?

Way#1: Model with a tape diagram

Way#2: Represent the problem using letters for the unknown quantity. Solve with numbers.

Explain your thinking:

PUT TOGETHER/TAKE APART—WHOLE UNKNOWN

5. John spent $55 dollars on shoes and $199 on clothes. He also spent $44 on socks and $56 on ties. How much money did he spend altogether?

Way#1: Solve with a number line

Way#2: Show all your mathematical thinking

Explain your thinking:

PUT TOGETHER/TAKE APART—WHOLE UNKNOWN

6. Sue left her house at 2:10 p.m. She spent 45 minutes at her aunt's house and 45 minutes at her grandmother's house. How long was she gone altogether? What time did she get back home?

Solve with a number line diagram

Explain your thinking:

Problem Solving with Math Models© 2012

PUT TOGETHER/TAKE APART - WHOLE UNKNOWN

7. Grandma Betsy used 234 grams of sugar in her cookie mix and 389 grams of sugar in her pie mix. How many grams of sugar did she use altogether?

Way#1: Model with a tape diagram

Way#2: Represent the problem using letters for the unknown quantity. Solve with numbers.

Explain your thinking:

PUT TOGETHER/TAKE APART—WHOLE UNKNOWN

8. Chef Rodriguez made a fancy fruit punch. He used 257 ml of apple juice, 345 ml of cranberry juice, 29 ml of pineapple juice, and 7 ml of orange juice. How many ml of juice did he make altogether?

Way#1: Model with a tape diagram

Way#2: Represent the problem using letters for the unknown quantity. Solve with numbers.

Explain your thinking:

Problem Solving with Math Models© 2012

CHAPTER 1 QUIZ: PUT TOGETHER/ TAKE APART – WHOLE UNKNOWN PROBLEMS

Solve with a model:

1. Lucy left her house at 12:23 p.m. She went to the mall for 1 hour and a half. She went to her cousin's for 25 minutes. How long was she gone? What time did she get home?

2. A yard is 7 ft. long and 8 ft. wide. What is the perimeter?

3. The toy store had 8 soccer balls, 3 footballs, 9 baseballs, 4 tennis balls, and 7 kickballs? How many balls did they have altogether?

4. The bakery had 45 chocolate cookies, 37 lemon ones, 18 strawberry ones, and 4 sugar ones. How many cookies did they have altogether?

CHAPTER 2
PUT TOGETHER/TAKE APART PROBLEMS PART UNKNOWN

These types of problems are about sets of things. In them, we know the total and one part of the set. We are looking for the other part of the set.

PROBLEM	John had ten apples. Five were red apples and the rest were green. How many apples were green?
MODEL	
EQUATION	$5 + ? = 10$ $\qquad\qquad 5 + 5 = 10$

PUT TOGETHER/TAKE APART - PART UNKNOWN

1. Farmer Kendra had 100 apple trees. Fifty-five of them grew red apples, twenty-three grew green and the rest grew yellow apples. How many grew yellow apples?

Way#1: Solve with a number line

Way#2: Show all your mathematical thinking

Explain your thinking:

PUT TOGETHER/TAKE APART - PART UNKNOWN

2. Tara spent $348. She spent $173 on clothes, $48 on shoes, $99 on jewelry, and the rest on perfume. How much did she spend on perfume?

Way#1: Model with a tape diagram

Way#2: Solve with numbers

Explain your thinking:

PUT TOGETHER/TAKE APART - PART UNKNOWN

3.   This weekend 3,459 people went to see comedies, 2,459 people went to see love stories and the rest went to see action movies. A total of 10,000 people went to the movies. How many people went to see action movies?

Way#1: Solve with an tape diagram

Way#2: Represent the problem using letters for the unknown quantity. Solve with numbers.

Explain your thinking:

PUT TOGETHER/TAKE APART - PART UNKNOWN

4.   The farm had 200 rabbits. Sixty-two of them had spots, seventy-five of them were all white, and the rest were black.   How many black rabbits were there?

Way#1: Solve with a number line

Way#2: Represent the problem using letters for the unknown quantity. Solve with numbers.

Explain your thinking:

PUT TOGETHER/TAKE APART - PART UNKNOWN

5.   Jose left his house at 4:23 p.m. He was gone for two hours. He spent 45 minutes at the mall. He spent the rest of the time at the playground. How long did he go to the playground?

Solve with a number line diagram

Explain your thinking:

Problem Solving with Math Models© 2012

PUT TOGETHER/TAKE APART - PART UNKNOWN

6. Terri left her house at 3:20 p.m. She was gone for 1 hour and a half. She spent 60 minutes in the mall and the rest of the time at her friend's house. How long did she spend at her friend's house?

Solve with a number line diagram

Explain your thinking:

Put Together/Take Apart—Part Unknown

7. Grandma Lara used 800 grams of sugar for her cookies. She used 555 grams in her sugar cookies and the rest in her chocolate chip cookies. How many grams did she use in her chocolate chip cookies?

Way#1: Model with a tape diagram

Way#2: Represent the problem using letters for the unknown quantity. Solve with numbers.

Explain your thinking:

PUT TOGETHER/TAKE APART - PART UNKNOWN

8. Andy made a great fruit punch. He used 900 ml of juice. He used 150 of pineapple juice, 250 ml of apple juice, 75 ml of cherry juice, 299 ml of orange juice and the rest was banana juice. How much was banana juice?

Way#1: Model with a tape diagram

Way#2: Represent the problem using letters for the unknown quantity. Solve with numbers.

Explain your thinking:

CHAPTER 2 QUIZ:
PUT TOGETHER/TAKE APART – PART UNKNOWN

Solve with a model:

1. Claire had $378. She spent $8 on earrings, $43 on necklaces, $235 on clothes, and the rest on shoes. How much did she spend on shoes?

2. Jackson built a fence. The perimeter was 34 ft. The length was 7 ft. What was the width?

Problem Solving with Math Models© 2012

3. Jason drank 1000 ml of milk. He drank 246 ml of plain milk, 345 ml of chocolate milk, and the rest was strawberry milk. How much strawberry milk did he drink?

4. Jenny had 36 inches of string. She used 12 inches on Monday, 8 inches on Tuesday, and the rest on Wednesday. How much string did she use on Wednesday?

Unit 3 Test:
Put Together/Take Apart

Solve with a model:

1. The fruit stand had 15 kilos of yellow apples and 17 kilos of red apples. It also had 18 kilos of green apples. How many kilos of apples did it have altogether?

2. Don mixed 589 ml of pineapple juice with some ml of grape juice to make his famous fruit punch. He mixed 1000 ml of juice altogether. How much grape juice did he mix in to the punch?

3.   The perimeter of the lawn was 30 ft. The length was 8 ft. How long was the width?

4.   Rudy left his house at 3:10 p.m. He was gone for 2 hours and 15 minutes. He spent 70 minutes at the mall. He spent the rest of the time at his grandmother's house. How long was he at his grandmother's house?

CHAPTER 1
COMPARE DIFFERENCE UNKNOWN

In these problems, students are comparing two or more amounts. They are comparing to find out what the difference is between the amounts. There are two versions of this type of story. One version uses the word "more" and one version uses the word "fewer." The version with the word "fewer" is considered to be more difficult.

PROBLEM MORE VERSION	John had 12 marbles. Carl had 2 marbles. How many more marbles does John have than Carl?
MODEL	
EQUATION	2 + ? = 12 2 + 10 = 12

PROBLEM FEWER VERSION	Carl had 2 marbles. John had 12 marbles. How many fewer marbles does Carl have than John?
MODEL	
EQUATION	12 − 2 = ? 12 − 2 = 10

COMPARE FRACTIONS

1. John ate ½ of a small pizza. Kurt ate ¼ of a small pizza? If the pizzas were the same size, who ate more?

Way#1: Solve with pictures

Way#2: Solve with a number line

Explain your thinking:

COMPARE FRACTIONS

2. Tommy ate 5/6 of his candy bar. Kayla at 6/6 of hers. Who ate more if the candy bars were the same size?

Way#1: Solve with a number line

Way#2: Show the relationship using the symbols
     <, >, =

Explain your thinking:

COMPARE FRACTIONS

3.   Jose jogged 2/4 of a mile this morning. Tom jogged 1/2 of a mile this afternoon. Who ran farther?

Solve with a number line

Explain your thinking:

COMPARE USING GRAPHS

4.	Favorite Ice Cream Flavors
Vanilla	9
Chocolate	15
Strawberry	12
Cherry	10

Draw a scaled bar graph to represent the data

Question 1: How many people voted altogether?

Question 2: How many more people like chocolate than cherry?

Question 3: How many fewer people like vanilla than strawberry?

Problem Solving with Math Models© 2012

COMPARE USING GRAPHS

5.	Favorite Sports
Soccer	25
Football	19
Basketball	27
Baseball	31

Draw a scaled bar graph to represent the data

Question 1: How many people voted altogether?

Question 2: How many more people like basketball than football?

Question 3: How many fewer people like football than soccer?

COMPARE DIFFERENCE UNKNOWN

6. Grandma Betty used 525 grams of sugar in her sugar cookies. She used 439 grams of sugar in her lemon cookies. How much less sugar did she use in her lemon cookies than she did in her sugar cookies?

Way#1: Solve with a double number line

Way#2: Show all your mathematical thinking

Explain your thinking:

Problem Solving with Math Models© 2012

COMPARE DIFFERENCE UNKNOWN

7. In one hour on the internet, 7,800 people like Video A, but only 4,598 people liked Video B. How many more people liked Video A than liked Video B? How many people voted altogether for the videos?

Way#1: Model with a tape diagram

Way#2: Show all your mathematical thinking

Explain your thinking:

COMPARE DIFFERENCE UNKNOWN

8. Mrs. Joseph's garden has a length of 4 ft. and a width of 5 ft. Mrs. Lucy's garden has a length of 5 ft. and a width of 6 ft. Whose garden has the larger perimeter? How much larger is the perimeter of the larger garden than the smaller one?

Way#1: Solve with a drawing

Way#2: Solve with numbers

Explain your thinking:

CHAPTER 1 QUIZ: COMPARE PROBLEMS

Solve with a model:

1. In 1 hour, 5,555 people liked Song A on the Internet. Only 4,578 people liked Song B. How many more people liked Song A than liked Song B? How many people voted altogether?

2. Mr. Jamal planted 2 gardens. Garden A had a length of 7 ft. and a width of 8 ft. Garden B had a length of 5 ft. and a width of 15 ft. Which garden had a larger perimeter? How much larger was the perimeter of the larger garden than the smaller garden?

COMPARE USING GRAPHS

3.	Favorite Cookies
Lemon	34
Sugar	28
Chocolate Chip	55
Peanut Butter	19
Other	37

Draw a scaled picture graph to represent the data

Question 1: How many people voted altogether?

Question 2: How many more people like chocolate chip than lemon?

Question 3: How many people's choices were not on the chart?

Question 4: Make up a question you could ask about the chart.

Problem Solving with Math Models© 2012

COMPARE DIFFERENCE UNKNOWN

4. Kayla ate 1/5 of her candy bar. Luke at 5/5 of his candy bar. Who ate more if the candy bars were the same size?

Way#1: Draw a picture to solve

Way#2: Compare these two fractions with symbols >, <, or =

Explain your thinking:

CHAPTER 2
COMPARISON – BIGGER PART UNKNOWN

In these problems, students are comparing two or more amounts. They are comparing to find out who had the bigger part. There are two versions of this type of story. One version uses the word "more" and one version uses the word "fewer." The version with the word "fewer" is considered to be more difficult.

PROBLEM MORE VERSION	John has 5 more marbles than Carl. Carl has 2 marbles. How many marbles does John have?
MODEL	 7 total John Carl
EQUATION	2 + 5 = ? 2 + 5 = 7

PROBLEM FEWER VERSION	Carl has 3 fewer marbles than John? Carl has 2 marbles. How many marbles does John have?
MODEL	 Carl John 5 total
	2 + 3 = ? 2 + 3 = 5

COMPARISON – BIGGER PART UNKNOWN

1. Dan has 35 marbles. David has ten more than he does. How many does David have? How many do they have altogether?

Way#1: Model with a tape diagram

Way#2: Show all your mathematical thinking

Explain your thinking:

COMPARISON – BIGGER PART UNKNOWN

2. Grandma Betsy used 289 grams of sugar in her lemon pie and 100 more grams of sugar in her blackberry pie. How many grams of sugar did she use in her blackberry pie? How many grams of sugar did she use altogether?

Way #1: Solve with a double number line

Way #2: Represent the problem using letters for the unknown quantity. Solve with numbers.

Explain your thinking:

COMPARISON – BIGGER PART UNKNOWN

3. Emily had 25 marbles. Carlos had 15 more than she did. Maya had 10 less than Carlos. How many marbles did Carlos have? How many did Maya have? How many do they have altogether?

Way#1: Model with a tape diagram

Way#2: Show all your mathematical thinking

Explain your thinking:

COMPARISON – BIGGER PART UNKNOWN

4. The toy store has 55 tennis balls. There are 18 more soccer balls than tennis balls. How many soccer balls are there? How many balls are there altogether?

Way#1: Solve with a double number line

Way#2: Represent the problem using letters for the unknown quantity. Solve with numbers.

Explain your thinking:

Problem Solving with Math Models© 2012

COMPARISON – BIGGER PART UNKNOWN

5. The ice cream store has 133 fudge popsicles. There are 56 more ice cream sandwiches than popsicles. How many ice cream sandwiches are there?

Way#1: Solve with a double number line

Way#2: Represent the problem using letters for the unknown quantity. Solve with numbers.

Explain your thinking:

COMPARISON – BIGGER PART UNKNOWN

6. On the Internet, Song A got 7,891 votes in 1 hour. Song B got 1,348 more votes than Song A. How many votes did Song B get? How many people voted altogether?

Way#1: Solve with a double number line

Way#2: Represent the problem using letters for the unknown quantity. Solve with numbers.

Explain your thinking:

Problem Solving with Math Models© 2012

COMPARISON – BIGGER PART UNKNOWN

7. The toy store has 59 red marbles, 32 multicolored marbles, and 49 black marbles. There are ten more green marbles than black marbles. There are twenty more purple marbles than the red and multicolored marbles combined. How many green marbles are there? How many purple marbles are there? How many marbles are there in total?

Way#1: Model with a tape diagram

Way #2: Represent the problem using letters for the unknown quantity. Solve with numbers.

Explain your thinking:

COMPARISON – BIGGER PART UNKNOWN

8. Craig drank 756 ml of orange juice. He drank 100 fewer ml than Jose? How many ml of orange juice did Jose drink?

Way#1: Solve with a double number line

Way#2: Represent the problem using letters for the unknown quantity. Solve with numbers.

Explain your thinking:

Chapter 2 Quiz:
Comparison Bigger Part Unknown

Solve with a model:

1. John has 57 marbles. Steve has 23 more marbles than John. How many marbles does Steve have? How many marbles do they have altogether?

2. Song A has 4,567 votes. It has 3,459 fewer votes than Song B. How many votes does Song B have?

3. The bakery used 789 grams of sugar for cookies and 178 more grams for doughnuts. How many grams of sugar did it use for doughnuts? How many grams of sugar did it use altogether?

4. Harry drank 508 ml of water. His brother drank 100 more than he did. His cousin drank 358 more ml than his brother did. How much did his brother drink? How much did his cousin drink?

CHAPTER 3
COMPARISON – SMALLER PART UNKNOWN

In these problems, students are comparing two or more amounts. They are comparing to find out who has the smaller amount. There are two versions of this type of story. One version uses the word "more" and one version uses the word "fewer". The version with the word "more" is considered to be more difficult.

PROBLEM MORE VERSION	John had 4 more marbles than Carl. John had 5 marbles. How many marbles did Carl have?
MODEL	John ⬤ ⬤ ⬤ ⬤⬤ Carl ⬤
EQUATION	5 - 4 = ? 5 – 4 = 1

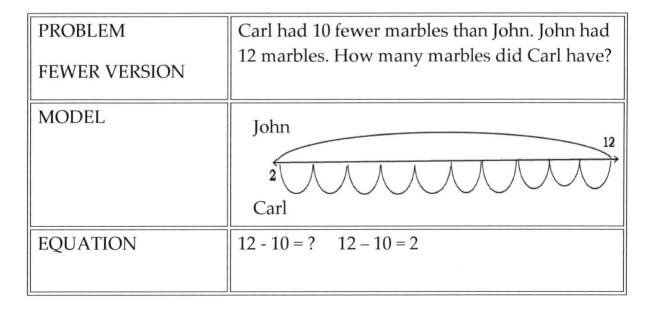

PROBLEM FEWER VERSION	Carl had 10 fewer marbles than John. John had 12 marbles. How many marbles did Carl have?
MODEL	
EQUATION	12 - 10 = ? 12 – 10 = 2

COMPARISON – SMALLER PART UNKNOWN

1. Luke drank 500 ml of orange juice for breakfast. Julian drank 18 ml less than he did. How many ml did Julian drink?

Way#1: Solve with a drawing.

Way#2: Represent the problem using letters for the unknown quantity. Solve with numbers.

Explain your thinking:

COMPARISON – SMALLER PART UNKNOWN

2. Amanda has 9 pies. Melissa has 3 less than she does. Kayla has 5 more than Melissa does. How many pies does Kayla have?

Way#1: Solve with pictures

Way#2: Solve with numbers

Explain your thinking:

COMPARISON – SMALLER PART UNKNOWN

3.   Song A has 5,678 downloads. Song B has 3,789 fewer downloads than Song A. How many downloads does Song B have?

Way#1: Solve with a tape diagram

Way#2: Solve with numbers

Explain your thinking:

Problem Solving with Math Models© 2012

COMPARISON – SMALLER PART UNKNOWN

4. The bookstore has 22 butterfly bookmarks. It has 15 fewer sports bookmarks. How many sports bookmarks does it have? How many bookmarks does it have altogether?

Way#1: Solve with tape diagram

Way#2: Solve with numbers

Explain your thinking:

COMPARISON – SMALLER PART UNKNOWN

5. Mr. Robinson planted 2 gardens. Garden A had a length of 4 ft. and a width of 5 ft. The length of Garden B was 1 ft. smaller and the width of Garden B was 2 ft. smaller. What was the perimeter of Garden A? What was the perimeter of Garden B?

Way#1: Solve with a drawing

Way#2: Solve with numbers

Explain your thinking:

COMPARISON – SMALLER PART UNKNOWN

6. The bakery had 55 sugar cookies. They had 10 fewer lemon cookies than sugar cookies and 7 fewer vanilla cookies than lemon. How many lemon cookies did they have? How many vanilla cookies did they have?

Way#1: Model with a tape diagram

Way#2: Solve with numbers

Explain your thinking:

COMPARISON – SMALLER PART UNKNOWN

7. Luke's grandma gave him $100 for his birthday. His sister gave him $20 less than his grandmother and his brother gave him $7 less than his sister did. How much did his sister give him? How much did his brother give him?

Way#1: Model with a tape diagram

Way#2: Show all your mathematical thinking

Explain your thinking:

COMPARISON – SMALLER PART UNKNOWN

8. Mary made fruit punch. She added 859 ml of orange juice. She put in 398 fewer ml of pineapple juice. She put in 108 fewer ml of apple juice than pineapple juice. How much pineapple juice did she add? How much apple juice did she add?

Way#1: Model with a tape diagram

Way#2: Solve with numbers

Explain your thinking:

CHAPTER 3 QUIZ:
COMPARISON SMALLER UNKNOWN PROBLEMS

Solve with a model:

1.   The jewelry store had 123 silver rings. They had 48 fewer gold rings than silver ones. They had 20 fewer wooden rings than gold ones. How many gold rings did they have? How many wooden rings did they have?

2.   Sue jogged ¼ of a mile. Tom jogged 1/3 of a mile who jogged farther?

Problem Solving with Math Models© 2012

3. Jamal had $204. He went to the mall and bought $129 worth of clothes. He spent $59 less on shoes. How much did he spend on shoes? How much did he spend altogether?

4. Chef Lou made 2,584 ml of fresh orange juice. He then made 257 ml less of fresh apple juice. How much apple juice did he make?

Unit 4 Test:
Compare Problems

Solve with a model:

1. Sue ate 2/3 of her candy bar. Joe at 3/3 of his. If the candy bars were the same size, who ate more?

2. Grandma Luz used 459 grams of flour in her strawberry cake and 100 more grams in her lemon cake. How many grams did she use in her lemon cake? How many grams of sugar did she use for both cakes?

3. Mr. Garcia planted 2 gardens. Garden A was a square garden with a perimeter of 40 ft. Garden B was a rectangle. The length of Garden B was 3 feet shorter than Garden A. The width stayed the same. What was the length of Garden B? What was the perimeter of Garden B?

4. Mary went shopping. She spent $34 on perfume. She spent $10 more than that on a scarf. She spent $20 less on the earrings than on the scarf. How much did the scarf cost? How much did the earrings cost?

Compare Using Graphs:

5.	Favorite Types of Movies
Comedy	95
Action	99
Horror	68
Romance	85

Draw a scaled picture graph to represent the data

Question 1: How many people voted altogether?

Question 2: How many more people like comedy than romance?

Question 3: How many fewer people liked horror than action?

Question 4: What is another question you could ask about the data in the graph?

6. Marcos had 55 more marbles than Tom. Tom had 79 marbles. Luke had 10 fewer marbles than Marcos. How many did Marcos have? How many marbles did Luke have?

Compare Using Graphs:

7.	Favorite Types of Stuffed Animals
Bears	52
Elephants	48
Rabbits	34
Other	78

Draw a scaled picture graph to represent the data

Question 1: How many people voted altogether?

Question 2: How many more people liked bears than rabbits?

Question 3: How many fewer people like rabbits than elephants?

Question 4: What is another question you could ask about the data in the graph?

CHAPTER 1
MULTISTEP WORD PROBLEMS

There are 5 types of CCSS two-step problems. In these problems, either the steps involve the same operation, two different operations, or a mixture of different problem types. Throughout this chapter, we will practice each type.

Multi-Step/Different Operations

PROBLEM	There were 5 comic books and 2 sports books on the shelf. Susie put 2 more comic books on the shelf. How many books are there on the shelf now?
MODEL	
EQUATIONS	5 + 2 = 7 7 + 2 = 9

PROBLEM	There were 5 books on the table. John took 3 books. Sue put 7 more books on the table. How many books are on the table now?
MODEL	
EQUATIONS	5 - 3 = 2 2 + 7 = 9

Multi-Step/Different Problem Types

PROBLEM	Sue had 5 candies. Terri had 2 more candies than Sue. How many candies did they have altogether?
MODEL	
EQUATIONS	5 + 2 = 7 5 + 7 = 12

Multi-Step/Mixed Problem Types

PROBLEM	There were 5 comic books and some sports books on a shelf. There were 10 books altogether. Sue put 2 more sports books on the shelf. How many sports books are there now?
MODEL	
EQUATIONS	5 + ? = 10 5 + 5 = 10 10 + 2 = 7

Multi-Step/Different Operations

PROBLEM	There were 3 red marbles and some green marbles on the table. There were 5 marbles in all. Then Sue put some more green marbles on the table and now there are 10 green marbles on the table. How many green marbles did Sue put on the table?
MODEL	
EQUATIONS	3 + ? = 5 2 + ? = 10 2 + 8 = 10

MULTI-STEP/SAME OPERATION

Solve with a model:

1. Jose had 18 marbles. Marta gave him 12 more. Louis gave him 10 more. How many does he have now?

2. Mary had 53 marbles. Her brother gave her 18 more. Then her mom gave her 15 more. How many marbles does she have now?

3. Tom had 45 stickers. He gave 15 to his brother. Then he gave 10 to his sister. Now how many does he have?

4. Rogelio had 8 toy cars. He gave 1 to his brother, 2 to his sister and 1 to a friend. How many does he have left?

MULTI-STEP/MIXED OPERATIONS

Solve with a model:

1. Daniel had 47 stickers. His brother had 18 fewer than he did. How many do they have altogether?

2. Carlos had 34 marbles. His brother had 45 more than he did. How many marbles did they have altogether?

3. There were 15 green marbles and some yellow marbles in a bag. There were 20 marbles altogether. John put 25 more yellow marbles in the bag. How many yellow marbles are in the bag now?

4. Tommy had 15 toy cars and some toy trucks in the toy box. He had 25 toy vehicles in the box altogether. Then he put 5 more trucks in the toy box. How many toy trucks does he have now?

5.   In a ball box, there were 8 footballs and some soccer balls. In total, there were 14 balls in the box. Then Jamal put some more soccer balls in the box. Now there are 10 soccer balls in the box. How many soccer balls did Jamal put in the box?

6.   In a cookie jar, there were 55 peanut butter cookies and some lemon cookies. In total, there were 70 cookies in the cookie jar. Then Mrs. Brown put some more lemon cookies in the jar. Now there are 25 lemon cookies in the jar. How many lemon cookies did Mrs. Brown put in the jar?

7. There were 15 coconuts and 17 bananas in a display window at a fruit stand. Farmer Tom added 5 more coconuts and 7 more bananas. How many fruits are in the display window now?

8. There were 10 orange butterflies in the garden. There were 10 more green ones than orange ones. There were 5 fewer purple ones than green ones. How many butterflies were in the garden altogether?

UNIT 5 TEST:
MULTI-STEP WORD PROBLEMS

Solve with a model:

1. Jane had 25 stickers. Ten were animal stickers and the rest were doll stickers. Then her sister gave her 8 more doll stickers. How many doll stickers does Jane have now?

2. There were 17 orange marbles and some silver marbles in a bag. There were 20 marbles altogether in the bag. Miguel put some more silver marbles in the bag and now there are a total of 8 silver marbles. How many silver marbles did Miguel put in the bag?

3. Joe had 18 candies. He gave his brother 5 and his sister gave him 2. His mom gave him 11 more candies. How many candies does he have now?

4. The bakery made 53 lemon cupcakes in the morning. In the afternoon, they made 30 more chocolate ones than the lemon ones. They made 10 fewer strawberry ones than chocolate ones. How many cupcakes did they make altogether?

NAME:

DATE:

Solve the problems. Show your thinking by drawing a picture, using a number line, or making a table.

1. Luke left his house at 3:15 p.m. He spent an hour at Brian's house and an hour at the basketball court. What time did he come home?

2. Carol the baker used 47 grams of sugar in her cake mix. Then she added 88 more grams of sugar. How many grams of sugar did she put in altogether?

3. Farmer Jane built a yard for her rabbits. First, she made a yard that was 7ft long and 7 ft. wide. Then she added some fence to the length. Now the length is 10 ft. long. How much fence did she add to the length? What is the new perimeter of the yard?

4. The school cook made some liters of fruit punch. He then made 12 more liters. Altogether he made 50 liters of fruit punch. How much fruit punch did he have in the beginning?

5. Sara had 305 cm of string to make bracelets. She used 98 cm on Monday, 36 cm on Tuesday, 48 cm on Wednesday, and 104 cm on Thursday. How much string did she have left on Friday?

6. Jose left his house at 3:15 p.m. He came back at 4:55 p.m. How long was he gone?

7. The candy store sold 9 kilograms of chocolate in the morning, 18 kilograms in the afternoon, and some more in the evening. Altogether they sold 32 kilograms of chocolate. How many kilograms did they sell in the evening?

8. The clothing store had some dresses. They sold 28 dresses on Monday, 38 on Tuesday, and 48 on Wednesday. Now they have 18 left. How many dresses did they have to start?

9. Ten thousand people went to the movies this weekend. 4,459 people went to see comedies, 2,459 people went to see love stories and the rest went to see action movies. How many people went to see action movies?

10. Justin built a fence with a perimeter of 48 ft. The length was 12 feet. What was the width?

11. Tommy ate 2/6 of his candy bar. Kayla at 6/6 of hers. If the candy bars were the same size, who ate more?

Compare Using Graphs:

12.	Favorite Shows
Drama	35
Sports	55
Comedies	50
News	45

Draw a picture graph to represent the data.

Question 1: How many people voted altogether?

Question 2: How many more people like sports shows than drama shows?

Question 3: How many fewer people like the news than like comedies?

Question 4: What is another question that you can ask about this graph?

Problem Solving with Math Models© 2012

13. Grandma Rachel used 389 grams of sugar in her peach pie and 100 more grams of sugar in her plum pie. How many grams of sugar did she use in her plum pie? How many grams of sugar did she use altogether?

Compare Using Graphs:

14.	Favorite Types of Pets
Lizards	20
Dogs	70
Cats	60
Fish	40
Other	60

Draw a scaled picture graph to represent the data

Question 1: How many people voted altogether?

Question 2: How many more people like dogs than lizards?

Question 3: How many fewer people liked lizards than cats?

Question 4: What is another question you could ask about the data in the graph?

Problem Solving with Math Models© 2012

15. In the ball box, there were 5 footballs and some soccer balls. In total, there were 10 balls in the box. Then James put some more soccer balls in the box. Now there are 12 soccer balls in the box. How many soccer balls did James put in the box?

16. There were 12 purple marbles and some blue marbles in the bag. There were 20 marbles altogether. John put 25 more blue marbles in the bag. How many blue marbles are in the bag now?

17. On the Internet, Song A got 5,091 votes in 1 hour. Song B got 4,348 more votes than Song A. How many votes did Song B get? How many people voted altogether?

18. Mr. Richards planted 2 gardens. Garden A had a length of 5 ft. and a width of 5 ft. The length of Garden B was 1 ft. smaller and the width of Garden B was 2 ft. smaller. What was the perimeter of Garden A? What was the perimeter of Garden B?

19. Luke's grandma gave him $200 for his birthday. His sister gave him $50 less than his grandmother did. His brother gave him $77 less than his sister did. How much did his sister give him? How much did his brother give him?

UNIT 1

Chapter 1: Add to Result Unknown Problems
1. 50 marbles
2. 4:15 p.m.
3. 85 grams
4. 99 ml
5. 75 ml
6. 837 grams
7. 13 ft. long; 36 ft.
8. 319 inches

Chapter 1 Quiz: Add to Results Unknown
1. 1:45
2. 36 ft
3. 921 gumballs
4. 34 kilograms

Chapter 2: Add to Change Unknown Problems
1. 15 marbles
2. 1 hour
3. 250 grams
4. 500 ml
5. 18 stickers
6. 52 centimeters
7. 4 ft.; 32 ft.
8. 53 action figures

Chapter 2 Quiz: Add to Change Unknown Problem
1. 57 ml
2. 24 kilograms
3. 15 cupcakes
4. 1 hour

Chapter 3: Add to Start Unknown
1. 15 gummy bears
2. 12:15 p.m.
3. 15 feet
4. 25 kilograms
5. 38 liters
6. 33 marbles
7. 8 kilograms
8. 45 stuffed animals

Chapter 3 Quiz: Add to Start Unknown Problems
1. 106 centimeters
2. 7:25 a.m.
3. 151 ml
4. 2 kilometers

UNIT 1 TEST: ADDITION PROBLEMS
1. 232 rings
2. 13 marbles
3. 18 cookies
4. 155 grams

Unit 2

Chapter 1: Take From Result Unknown

1. $50
2. 3 kilograms
3. 19 cm
4. 48 stamps
5. 168 pages
6. 15 minutes
7. 75 ml
8. 12 feet

Chapter 1 Quiz: Take From Result Unknown Problems (pp. 60-61)

1. 55 cookies
2. 7 kilograms
3. 42 centimeters
4. $8

Chapter 2: Take From Change Unknown Problems

1. 4 kilos
2. 1 hour, 15 minutes
3. 2 hours, 40 minutes
4. 11 kilos
5. 38 cm; 242 CM
6. 8 ft.; 34 ft.
7. 3 ft.; 20 ft.
8. $47; $19

Chapter 2 Quiz: Take From Change Unknown Problems

1. 8 marbles; 67 left
2. 8 kilos
3. 2 hours, 5 minutes
4. $27; $9

Chapter 3: Take From Start Unknown Problems

1. $133
2. 150 ml
3. 96 cookies
4. 116 sweaters
5. 84 marbles
6. 100 cm
7. 42 kilos
8. $79

Chapter 3 Quiz: Take From Start Unknown Problems

1. 17 rings
2. 299 ml
3. 890 grams
4. $193

UNIT 2 TEST: TAKE FROM PROBLEMS

1. 88 marbles
2. $311
3. 19 rings; 12
4. 2:45 p.m.

UNIT 3

Chapter 1: Put Together/Take Apart— Whole Unknown Problems

1. 286 vehicles
2. 26 ft.
3. 4 hours, 15 minutes; 7:45
4. 23 miles
5. $354
6. 90 minutes; 3:40
7. 623 grams
8. 638 ml

Chapter 1 Quiz: Put Together/Take Apart—Whole Unknown Problems

1. 1 hour, 55 minutes; 2:18
2. 30 ft.
3. 31 balls
4. 104 cookies

Chapter 2: Put Together/Take Apart—Part Unknown Problems

1. 22 yellow apple trees
2. $28
3. 4,082 people
4. 63 rabbits
5. 1 hour, 15 minutes;
6. 30 minutes
7. 245 grams
8. 126 ml

Chapter 2 Quiz: Put Together/Take Apart—Part Unknown Problems

1. $92
2. 10 ft.
3. 409 ml
4. 16 inches

Unit 3 Test
Put Together/Take Apart Problems

1. 50 kilos of apples
2. 411 ml
3. 7 ft.
4. 1 hour and 5 min.

UNIT 4

Chapter 1: Compare Fractions Problems

1. John
2. Kayla
3. They ran the same amount

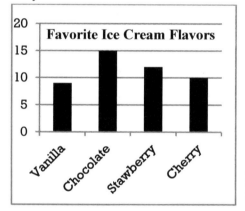

4.

Question 1: 46 people
Question 2: 5 people
Question 3: 3 people

5.

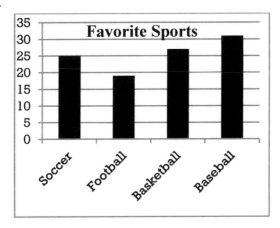

Favorite Sports

Question 1: 102 people
Question 2: 8 people
Question 3: 6 people

6. 86 grams
7. 3,202 more people; 12,398 people
8. Mrs. Lucy; 4 feet larger

Chapter 1 Quiz: Compare Difference

1. 977 more people; 10,133 people
2. Garden B; 10 ft. larger
3.

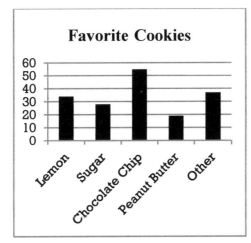

Favorite Cookies

Question 1: 173 people
Question 2: 21 more people
Question 3: 37 people
Question 4: Answers will vary

4. Luke

Chapter 2: Comparison—Bigger Part Unknown Problems

1. 45 marbles; 80 marbles
2. 389 grams; 678 grams
3. 40 marbles; 30 marbles; 95 marbles
4. 73 soccer balls; 128 balls
5. 189 ice cream sandwiches
6. 9,239 votes; 17,130 people
7. 59 green marbles; 111 purple marbles; 310 marbles altogether
8. 856 ml

Chapter 2 Quiz: Comparison—Bigger Part Unknown Problems

1. 80 marbles; 137 marbles
2. 8,026 votes
3. 967 grams; 1,756 grams
4. 608 ml; 966 ml

Chapter 3: Comparison—Smaller Part Unknown Problems

1. 482 ml
2. 11 pies
3. 1,889 downloads
4. 7 sports bookmarks; 29 bookmarks
5. 18 ft.; 12 ft.
6. 45 lemon; 38 vanilla
7. $80; $73
8. 461 ml; 353 ml

Chapter 3 Quiz: Comparison Smaller Unknown Problems

1. 75 gold rings; 55 wooden rings
2. Tom
3. $70; $199
4. 2,327 ml

UNIT 4 TEST: COMPARE PROBLEMS

1. Joe
2. 559 grams; 1,018 grams
3. 7 ft.; 34 ft.
4. $44; $24

UNIT 4 TEST: COMPARE PROBLEMS

1. Joe
2. 559 grams; 1,018 grams
3. 7 ft.; 34 ft.
4. $44; $34

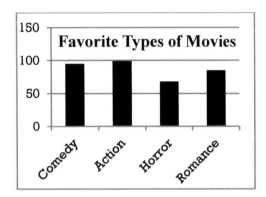

Question 1: 347 people
Question 2: 10 people
Question 3: 31 people
Question 4: Answers will vary

6. 134 marbles; 124 marbles
7.

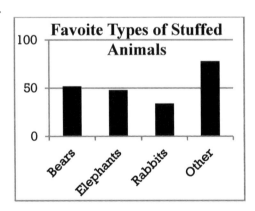

Question 1: 212 people
Question 2: 18 people
Question 3: 14 people
Question 4: Answers will vary

UNIT 5

Multi-step/Same Operation Problems

1. 40 marbles
2. 86 marbles
3. 20 stickers
4. 4 toy cars

Multi-step/Mixed Operations Problems

1. 76 stickers
2. 113 marbles
3. 30 yellow marbles
4. 15 toy trucks
5. 4 soccer balls
6. 10 lemon cookies
7. 44 fruits
8. 45 butterflies

UNIT 5 TEST: MULTI-STEP WORD PROBLEMS

1. 23 doll stickers
2. 5 silver marbles
3. 26 candies
4. 209 cupcakes

FINAL WORD PROBLEM TEST—THIRD GRADE

1. 5:15
2. 135 grams
3. 3 ft.; 34 ft.
4. 38 liters
5. 19 cm
6. 1 hour, 40 minutes
7. 5 kilograms
8. 132 dresses
9. 3,082 people
10. 12 ft
11. Kayla

12.

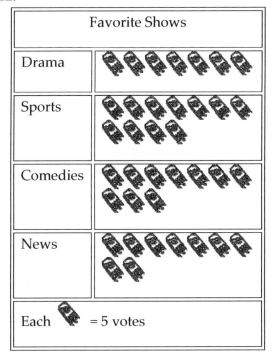

Favorite Shows	
Drama	🎬🎬🎬🎬🎬🎬🎬
Sports	🎬🎬🎬🎬🎬🎬🎬🎬🎬🎬🎬
Comedies	🎬🎬🎬🎬🎬🎬🎬🎬🎬
News	🎬🎬🎬🎬🎬🎬🎬🎬
Each 🎬 = 5 votes	

Question 1: 185 people
Question 2: 20 people
Question 3: 5 people
Question 4: Answers will vary

13. 489 grams; 878 grams

14.

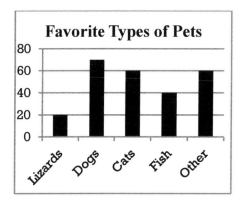

Favorite Types of Pets

Question 1: 250 people
Question 2: 50 people
Question 3: 40 people
Question 4: Answers will vary

15. 7 soccer balls
16. 33 blue marbles
17. 9,439 votes; 14,530 people
18. 20 ft; 14 ft
19. $150; $73

REFERENCES

Carpenter, T., Fennema, E., Franke, M., Levi, L., & Empson, S. (1999). *Children's Mathematics: Cognitively Guided Instruction.* Portsmouth, NH: Heinemann.

Charles, R. *Solving Word Problems: Developing Students' Quantitative Reasoning Abilities* http://assets.pearsonschool.com/asset_mgr/legacy/200931/Problem%20Solving%20Monograph_24324_1.pdf

Common Core Standards Writing Team (Bill McCullum, lead author). (2012, June 23). *Progressions for the common core state standards in mathematics: Geometry (draft).* Retrieved from: www.commoncoretools.wordpress.com.

Common Core Standards Writing Team (Bill McCullum, lead author). (2012, June 23). *Progressions for the common core state standards in mathematics: Geometric measurement (draft).* Retrieved from: www.commoncoretools.wordpress.com.

Common Core Standards Writing Team (Bill McCullum, lead author). (2011, June 20). *Progressions for the common core state standards in mathematics: K-3, Categorical data; Grades 2-5, Measurement Data (draft).* Retrieved from: www.commoncoretools.wordpress.com.

Common Core Standards Writing Team (Bill McCullum, lead author). (2011, May 29). *Progressions for the common core state standards in mathematics: K, Counting and cardinality; K-5, operations and algebraic thinking (draft).* Retrieved from: www.commoncoretools.wordpress.com.

Common Core Standards Writing Team (Bill McCullum, lead author). (2011, April 7). *Progressions for the common core state standards in mathematics: K-5, Number and operations in base ten (draft).* Retrieved from: www.commoncoretools.wordpress.com.

Common Core Standards Writing Team (Bill McCullum, lead author). (2011, July 12). *Progressions for the common core state standards in mathematics: 3-5 Number and operations - fractions (draft).* Retrieved from: www.commoncoretools.wordpress.com.

Peterson, P. L., Carpenter, T. P., & Loef, M. (1989). *Teachers' Pedagogical Content Beliefs in Mathematics. Cognition and Instruction,* Vol. 6, No. 1, pp. 1-40.

Made in the USA
Lexington, KY
22 August 2015